IRREGULAR MARRIAGES IN LONDON BEFORE 1754

by
Tony Benton

SOCIETY OF GENEALOGISTS
2000

First published by Society of Genealogists 1993

Second edition published by
Society of Genealogists Enterprises Limited,
14 Charterhouse Buildings
Goswell Road
London EC1M 7BA

ISBN 1 903462 05 3

Society of Genealogists Enterprises Limited is a wholly owned subsidiary of
Society of Genealogists, a registered charity, no. 233701

ABOUT THE AUTHOR

Tony Benton has had an active interest in local and family history since 1979.
He is a former member of the Executive Committee of the East of London
Family History Society, whose quarterly journal Cockney Ancestor he edited
from 1991 to 1995. He is author of many articles on family and local history
and of two Essex parish histories, Boldly from the marshes: a history of Little
Thurrock and its people (1992) and Upminster: the story of a garden suburb
(1996, with the late Albert Parish). His most recent books are Upminster and
Hornchurch in Old Photographs (1997) and The Changing Face of
Hornchurch (1999), both published by Sutton Publishing Ltd.

After gaining a Geography degree at Reading University, Tony worked in
personnel management for 17 years and now works in a senior position in
the Education Department of one of the Inner London boroughs. He and his
wife live in Upminster, Essex, and they have two children, a son at
University and a daughter studying A-levels.

CONTENTS

ILLUSTRATIONS

ACKNOWLEDGEMENTS

I have, where appropriate, in the notes on pp.50-55 below acknowledged the assistance of those who have helped in some way or other with this booklet, either in drawing my attention to or supplying references or in commenting on the text. I would like, in addition, to thank Stella Colwell at the Society of Genealogists for her careful copy editing of the first edition, Elizabeth Silverthorne for locating the etching used on the cover, Fred Banbery for his sketch of it; and Mark Herber for his helpful comments on the second edition. Any errors in the final work, of course, remain mine.

PREFACE TO FIRST EDITION

This booklet's origins can be traced back to my early days as a family historian in 1983 when I was faced with the problem of finding out more about my ancestor Aaron Benton. An unusual combination of forenames strongly suggested that Aaron and Frances Benton, parents of Mary baptised at South Ockendon, Essex in 1686, could be the same couple as 'Mr Aaron Benton and ... Frances his wife', parents of Aaron, 'borne and baptized ... in Starr Courte' in St Vedast Foster Lane in the City of London a year earlier. But how could the link between an Essex village and the City be found?

Eventually my background reading suggested a way forward. In the first volume of Don Steel's National Index of Parish Registers I found a section about London's lawless churches which in the seventeenth century 'arose to meet the popular demand for clandestine marriage'. This led me to the Guildhall Library where I soon found in the marriage register of Holy Trinity Minories the wedding of 'Aaron Benton widower of Upminster in Essex and Frances Harrison spinster of St Fosters' on 7 July 1684. The link was clear: Aaron junior was born in his mother's parish just over nine months later.

The South Ockendon register recorded the burial of Frances in January 1687/8, followed by a sequence of baptisms from 1689 for Aaron and Mary Benton, and a reference to Rebeccah Falkner, daughter of Mary 'now wife of Aaron Benton'. Again the Holy Trinity Minories register provided the answer – the wedding in July 1688 of 'Arron' Benton and Mary 'Foulkner'.

My first article on this subject, 'Clandestine marriage and the Minories', appeared in Cockney Ancestor, 21, Winter 1983/4, to be followed by further research, talks to local societies, and a more substantive article in the *Genealogists' Magazine* in March 1991. Shortly afterwards I was asked by Anthony Camp to expand my article to produce a booklet for the Society of Genealogists. This has finally seen the light of day.

PREFACE TO SECOND REVISED EDITION

The need to reprint this booklet has given me the chance to make some necessary amendments to the original text. Since it was published in 1993 there have been several important publications concerning clandestine marriage and the text has been updated to reflect this. Most textual amendments are in the chapter on marriage law where I have (I hope) given a clearer account of the position than in the first edition. The various graphs (Figures 2, 4, 6 and 7) have been redrawn and new and amended references, including some minor updating to details about the marriage centres, have been included in the Notes sections.

INTRODUCTION

In 1690 a Scottish visitor to London remarked on the 'privileged places' where weddings were performed after 'only taking an oath of the parties that they know just reason that might put a stop'.[1] Seven years later another visitor, the Frenchman Misson, commented that as early in the Morning as you please, Mr.Curate will marry them so fast that neither King nor Parliament can unmarry them; and for two Crowns your Business is dispatched. [2]

These visitors were describing a situation which has long been known to genealogists: the thriving trade in clandestine marriages which existed before Hardwicke's Marriage Act (26 Geo II c.31, 1753) came into effect in 1754. Burn described this in some detail in 1833 and others after him have added to the store of knowledge on this practice. Until recently the most widely-known reference was probably that in Don Steel's introductory volume of the National Index of Parish Registers, which drew heavily on Burn's original work supplemented by research by Roger Lee Brown, whose own work on clandestine marriages is perhaps little known by family historians. Within the past few years this topic has been more widely addressed.[3]

It is now almost thirty years since Steel commented that 'Records of Clandestine marriages are among the most important for the genealogist' and went on to note that 'unfortunate indeed is the searcher unable to fill at least one of his "blanks" from these sources'.[4]

This booklet looks at clandestine and irregular marriage in London in the century before Hardwicke's Marriage Act came into effect on 25 March 1754, and examines how genealogists and family historians can improve their chances of filling the 'blanks' on their trees.

MARRIAGE LAW

In theory, before Lord Hardwicke's Act of 1753, marriages were governed by the canons of the church approved in 1604. Amongst other things these canons, which largely codified existing regulations, ordered that marriages had to be carried out in as public a manner as possible between the hours of eight a.m. and noon in the parish church of either the bride or groom. Publicity of the proposed marriage was achieved by calling the banns in church on three successive Sundays or holy days or by obtaining a licence from the church authorities.

However, although the canons had been sanctioned by King James I, they were not backed up by Parliamentary legislation.[5] Under the laws of England, where there was a conflict between canon law and common law, the civil law of the country, it was canon law which submitted to the latter. Under the common law, marriages could still be valid even if some elements of canon law were not complied with.[6] So long as the couple clearly consented to the marriage and there was some proof of this, such as the confirmation by witnesses to their exchange of vows, in law there was no need for weddings to be performed by a clergyman to be regarded as valid.

Gillis has shown that until the early seventeenth century, the church was only partially successful in controlling marriage and 'ordinary people were still conducting a very large part of the business of marriage themselves'.[7] It was the public exchange of vows before witnesses, usually in an alehouse on market or feast day and often with a friend acting as the orator, which constituted the real marriage, rather than a ceremony performed in church by a clergyman. But the clergy's role progressively increased as first couples came to church to repeat their vows in the church porch, with the priest present to confirm that there were no hindrances. In later years a practice gradually evolved where the priests became more involved, acting as orators for the ceremony during which the couple placed their rings and coins on the priest's book. Betrothal was a joint promise to marry made by two people over the age of consent before two or more witnesses. Such vows were usually regarded as of a firmly binding nature and the betrothal, followed by consummation, remained for many the first step in the marriage process.

By the early sixteenth century it seems that most people later came to church to confirm their vows. The Puritan, Gouge, writing in 1622, regarded betrothed couples as 'in a middle degree betwixt single persons and married persons ... yea many take liberty after a contract to know their spouse, as if they were married: an unwarranted and dishonest practice'. The high rate of premarital pregnancy noted by many researchers confirms how common such sexual relations between betrothal and marriage were.[8] In some areas the betrothal process was known as 'handfasting' and the following example from Durham reveals the customary form of words and the formalities:

> After talke of agreiment the said Henry and Elizabeth wer contented ther in their presence to be handfested, which was done by Thomas Kingston, the said Henry Smith saying ... "Here I, Henry Smith, take you, Elizabeth Frissell, to my wedded wyf etc and thereto I plight the my trowth" ... drawing handes and drinking either to other.[9]

Although betrothal was usually considered as binding, many people changed their minds at a later stage, nevertheless, without losing face. The union could be dissolved, particularly if this was done publicly before witnesses. In the Lake District, for instance, such 'handfasts' could be terminated after a year and a day if both couples wished. However, the breaking of such promises sometimes resulted in actions brought before the church courts for breach of promise. Emmison's study of the church courts in Elizabethan Essex revealed over a hundred cases of disappointed parties who had sued for breach of a contract of matrimony.[10] Lawrence Stone's detailed examination of cases in the church courts gives ample evidence of the betrothal process, and of the participants' attitudes in such circumstances.[11]

Some historians define clandestine marriages as any which broke the church's restrictions and regulations laid down in canon law.[12] More recently Outhwaite has used the term 'irregular marriage' for those in breach of the church's canons. A common dictionary definition of clandestine is 'hidden or kept secret'. and a key element about clandestinity was that there had been some breach of the church's rules about publicity for the wedding. However, because the church failed to ensure that its canons were upheld, church discipline was largely non-existent by the early 1600s. A high proportion of marriages before 1754 might therefore be regarded either as irregular or clandestine, according to which definition is adopted.

9

Outhwaite has taken the view that clandestine marriage 'may have meant different things to different people at different times' and that in practice the terms clandestine and irregular might be regarded as more or less interchangeable[13]. Nevertheless it may be helpful to make a distinction according to the extent to which the marriages transgressed the church canons:–

- Firstly, was the abuse of banns certificates, either where a marriage took place in the parish of either bride or groom but without calling banns, or where banns were called but the wedding was performed away from the parish where they lived.

- A second category arose from the irregular use of the marriage licence. The canons of 1604 required marriages by licence to be celebrated 'publicly in the parish-church or chapel where one of them dwelleth, *and in no other place*'. Only a special licence from the Archbishop of Canterbury could dispense with this. A canon introduced in 1640 added the requirement that licences should only be granted if one of the couple had lived for at least a month within the area covered by the issuing ecclesiastical authority. But from the first half of the seventeenth century onwards, the first of these requirements was regularly ignored by the issuing church authorities, and there is considerable evidence of abuse of the latter restriction.

- A third category concerned marriages which took place without banns or licence in a church away from the parish of bride or groom, usually carried out by a properly ordained clergyman – this was the case at the two key London marriage venues of the last half of the seventeenth century, St James Duke's Place and Holy Trinity Minories. The church authorities' main objection to this practice was not so much that it transgressed canon law but that other clergymen and parishes were deprived of their rightful and lucrative marriage fees, as were those ecclesiastical officers empowered to issue marriage licences whose business was severely curtailed.

Although the above three categories were strictly outside canon law, at least they meant that some church authorities or clergy benefited from the wedding or licence fees. This was not the case with the fourth and final category:–

- Marriages which were not performed in any church or chapel, mainly those carried out in houses and taverns within the 'Rules' of the Fleet

Prison. Here the only beneficiaries were the Fleet parsons (usually, but not always, ordained men), the landlords who let out their premises for the ceremonies and the various hangers-on who owed their livelihood to this marriage trade.

Of these various categories only the third and fourth were truly *clandestine*. The other weddings, which were against canon law, but of which the church took a more permissive view, can best be regarded as *irregular*. Dr Patricia Kelvin has classified the different types of weddings as follows:[13]

	In parish of bride or groom?	
	Yes	No
By banns	Regular	Irregular
By licence	Regular	Irregular **
Neither	Irregular	Clandestine

** Regular if by special licence from the Archbishop of Canterbury.

In the account that follows I will only use the term *clandestine* to refer to marriages without banns or licence away from home parishes, and *irregular* to refer to other weddings which breached canon law in one way or other.

It was only when Hardwicke's Act 'for the Better Preventing of Clandestine Marriages' took effect on 25 March 1754, that the situation was clarified beyond doubt. The church canons and the statute law of the land were at last brought into line: thereafter, to be valid in the eyes of the law, all marriages had to be performed in the church or chapel in the parish where one of the partners lived, either after banns or by licence. The only exceptions were Jews and Quakers who had dispensation to conduct their own ceremonies; Nonconformists and Catholics, much to their displeasure, had to marry in the Church of England.

Hardwicke's Act formally required unions to be recorded in a separate register book of 'vellum or good and durable paper', with entries following a prescribed format, with spaces for standard details and signatures of the bride and groom and 'two or more credible witnesses'. This led to the registers consisting of bound volumes of printed forms, the now-familiar 'Hardwicke' registers.

THE SIXTEENTH AND EARLY SEVENTEENTH CENTURIES

Before the Reformation the various religious houses were outside the control of the church authorities. One of the accusations levied against them was that chaplains from these houses carried out clandestine ceremonies but, although this may have occurred, there is no evidence that this happened frequently. It seems that a significant move towards clandestine and irregular marriage originated in the period immediately after the Reformation when the chaplains of dissolved monasteries had not yet been brought effectively under the control of the bishops. It was probably during Edward VI's reign that the idea arose of benefiting from their independent position. Many such places then gained royal letters patent recognising their exemption from the bishops' authority: this is the origin of the so-called royal peculiars.

One of the earliest clandestine centres appears to have been the chapel of the Tower of London. Tomlinson refers to the fact that the chaplains at the Tower of London, which shared a similar exemption to the religious houses, claimed a right to marry all comers without banns or licence from the beginning of Edward VI's reign in 1547, probably aided and abetted by the Constables and Lieutenants of the Tower, who shared in the profits.[14] It seems that from 1623 marriages there were by licence only.

Evidently during the Elizabethan period there were widespread irregularities associated with marriage. Emmison records many examples from Essex of weddings by neither banns nor licence, unions performed in private houses, or carried out outside the canonical hours or within the 'closed' seasons. In the first category, for example, came Robert Marsh, Vicar of Great Wenden, summonsed to court in 1597 'for marrying one or two couples without banns thrice asking and without licence'. In addition Emmison offers evidence of an early clandestine centre: West Thurrock church, isolated in the Essex marshes near the sea wall and half a mile from the village it served, was 'called a lawless church'. Emmison cites the example from 1580 of Richard Bateman and his wife Joan from nearby South Ockendon, reprimanded for marrying at West Thurrock without banns or licence. Unfortunately the registers now only survive from 1680.[15]

I am not aware of any similarly detailed studies of life in Elizabethan London, but it is unlikely that there was significantly greater order in matrimonial matters in the metropolis. Certainly Jeremy Boulton has provided ample evidence that, during the early seventeenth century, irregular marriage, principally by licence, was extremely common in London, with City churches such as St Faith under St Paul and St Gregory by St Paul being the principal focus for this irregular trade.[16] At the latter church, Boulton has shown that 95% of weddings between 1599 and 1638 were by licence, almost half of these issued by the Faculty Office and over one-third by the Vicar General. This reflects the practice which re-emerged in the following century of marrying in a church adjacent to the office of the church official issuing the marriage licence. In fact Boulton suggests that the marriage customs in the capital before 1640 were 'symptoms of the later seventeenth century disease' (that is clandestine marriage). The church authorities in London seem deliberately to have relaxed the conditions surrounding marriage, by allowing officials and surrogates more freedom to issue licences. The moral was simple: this laxer discipline generated considerably more income for the ecclesiastical authorities.

According to Boulton's calculations, marriage by licence increased from about 7% of London weddings north of the Thames in 1550 to 18% in 1620 to a peak of almost 40% by 1640. There was a surge in the number of marriage licences issued in the 1620s and through the 1630s: on the eve of the Civil War the Bishop of London was issuing around 1,200 marriage licences each year, compared to an average of below 200 before 1620. Around the same time the Archbishop of Canterbury's Faculty Office issued around 1,000 licences annually. Much of the reason for this increase may have been because marriage by licence spread further down the social scale but it may also have been because marrying outside home parishes became more common. Boulton indicates that up to 65% of licences issued by the Bishop of London in 1640 were irregular, being issued for weddings outside the parish of both bride and groom.

The practice also spread to the area outside the City. At St Dunstan Stepney between 25% and 34% of weddings were by licence in the period 1618-1641. As this period went on the Bishop of London became the main issuing authority for licence weddings at Stepney, winning 'business' from the Faculty Office; at St Saviour Southwark over 45% of marriages were by licence. Before the Civil War, therefore, it was irregular rather than clandestine marriages which had made a significant impact on the London marriage market.[17]

It seems probable that after the outbreak of the Civil War in 1642 and the removal of the royal court and the bishops from London to Oxford, the abolition of the High Commission in 1641 and resulting collapse of the church courts and of the authorities' control was matched by the emergence of a truly clandestine marriage trade. It appears that Allhallows London Wall was acting as a clandestine or irregular centre from the 1640s and that around the same time a similar trade developed at St Thomas Southwark, where the number of weddings increased eightfold from around 15 a year between 1640-1643 to no less than 131 in 1646. Irregular marriage by licence however became less common: at St Peter Cornhill 71% of weddings in the decade before 1640 were by licence, but between 1641 and 1645 only around 15% were licensed weddings. At St Botolph Bishopsgate licensed weddings fell from 33% to 10% in the decades before and after 1640.

Stone suggests that because, at this time, the old marriage service according to the Book of Common Prayer had been declared 'popish' by the Puritan authorities, the legality of marriage ceremonies was unclear. Despite efforts to remedy this, the situation was only clarified by legislation passed by the Barebone's Parliament in 1653, which introduced civil marriage before a justice as the only legal form. Durston has indicated that many Londoners 'avoided the new secular ceremony by marrying between the passing of the Act in late August 1653 and the date when it came into force at the end of September'. A popular scandal sheet *Mercurius Democritus* reported that the city seamstresses had been unable to cope with the demand for bridal gowns! Wrigley and Schofield have calculated that the number of marriages in September 1653 was the highest monthly total during the 1650s, more than double the monthly average for the decade.[18]

Figure 1: The church of Holy Trinity Minories
Illustration: Guildhall Library, City of London
(with thanks to Mark Herber)

THE MINORIES AND DUKE'S PLACE

The parish of Holy Trinity Minories had been formed after the dissolution of the Priory of Holy Trinity during Henry VIII's onslaught on the monastic houses. The Priory's associated five acres of land within the parish of St Botolph Aldgate became a parish or precinct in its own right owned by the Crown, with the chapel of the Priory becoming the church of the new parish. The parishioners retained the sole right to appoint incumbents, without intervention of any other patron, and they successfully fought off attempts by the Bishop of London to establish the right of visitation there.

Although Tomlinson records that in 1641 the Bishop of London had been charged to visit Holy Trinity Minories 'to correct any abuses that may have arisen in the said chapel or its vicinity', there is no evidence from the parish register that clandestine weddings were carried out at that time; on average there were usually no more than twenty-five marriages a year recorded before 1644. The Minories marriage register indicates that the clandestine marriage trade seems to have begun there on 9 June 1644. On that date a new marriage register begins, and the level of register entries records a step-change in the number of weddings. Only 25 marriages are recorded in the five months between 1 January 1643/4 and 9 June 1644, but during the rest of the year 115 marriages were noted, with 249 in 1645 and between 348 and 368 in each of the next three years.[19]

Unfortunately the coverage of the registers at the Minories is very limited between 13 February 1648/9 until 26 March 1676, with only fragmentary registers surviving for the periods 17 February 1657/8 – 25 July 1659 and 30 April 1660 – 8 April 1663: the only complete calendar years are 1661 (532 marriages) and 1662 (397). It is probable that the need to be publicly married before a JP between 1654 and 1658 was marked by a suspension of the clandestine trade, but, in the absence of any surviving registers for the Minories, it is difficult to prove this.

However, the new civil form of marriage was unpopular as it went against popular custom and previous practice and clandestine marriages may have continued. Certainly the entries for the partial years 1658, 1659 and 1660 suggest that around 400 weddings a year were already taking place at the time of the Restoration, slightly higher than the level in 1648. By the time that the register sequence again resumes in 1676 the marriage trade at the Minories had more than doubled, with 759 weddings from 26 March to 31 December 1676, 967 marriages in 1677 and an annual average of 853 in the next five years.

Like other clandestine centres, St James Duke's Place founded its claim on its exemption from ecclesiastical control, in this case because the Lord Mayor and Citizens of London were the lords of the manor there. It is not clear when Duke's Place followed the example of its near-neighbour – I am unaware of any evidence to support Tomlinson's statement that Duke's Place and the Minories 'simultaneously ... made a beginning' by marrying without banns or licence in 1644. When the earliest surviving marriage register starts on 24 June 1665 the marriage trade was already well established with 797 weddings performed in the twelve months after that; in 1667 the register records 1,152 weddings.[20] This fragmentary register ends on 1 May 1668 while the main and virtually continuous register sequence only begins again on 6 March 1678/9. Therefore the record of over ten-thousand weddings between 1668 and 1678/9 has been lost, the register referring enquirers to 'the latter end of ye old book for what precedeth'.

The marriage register for Holy Trinity Minories between March 1676 and June 1683 contains 6,324 marriages (an annual average of almost 900), while the registers of Duke's Place for this period include around 1,700 weddings each year, about double the Minories level. In all, these two centres alone probably then accounted for over 2,500 weddings annually, perhaps around half of the weddings taking place in London at that period.[21]

The activities of these centres may have had a considerable effect on neighbouring parishes. My research suggests that people from the parishes on the fringe of the City, such as Stepney, were probably more than three times as likely to marry at the clandestine centres than in their home parish. For instance there were on average 110 marriages each year at St Dunstan Stepney between 1676 and 1680, yet at the Minories in 1677 there were 140 brides with Stepney named as their home parish. As the Duke's Place register at that time does not state abode, precise figures of Stepney folk marrying there cannot be assessed. However, as there were double the weddings at Duke's Place compared to the Minories, it is reasonable to assume that around 280 Stepney brides married there each year, giving a total of say 420 (or at worst a minimum of 400) Stepney brides at these two centres. This compares to at most 110 weddings in the parish of Stepney itself, not all of which involved Stepney people. This evidence suggests that just one in four weddings of Stepney folk took place in their home parish – a fact confirmed by Jeremy Boulton who shows that Stepney weddings between 1671 and 1680 only represented 28% of the level in the five years (1638 – 1642) before the Civil War. A similar pattern emerges in other parishes on the fringe of the City. Boulton's research shows an even more dramatic picture at St Giles Cripplegate and St Botolph Bishopsgate which in the same period recorded 16% and 20% respectively of the level of pre-Civil War unions. Perhaps one in five weddings are to be found in the registers of these home parishes (*see Figure 2*).

It is hardly surprising that the established church should attempt to stop this trade, if some parishes were losing fees for up to 80% of weddings. Action taken against St Botolph Aldgate in December 1684 *(see p. 21 below)* is one example showing that the authorities did not sit idly by; evidently this had a temporary effect on the Minories for between 17 December 1684 and 19 April 1685 only 13 weddings are recorded in the register (all by licence) instead of the 250 or so which might have been expected.

Figure 2: Weddings at St Giles Cripplegate illustrate trends in the seventeenth-century London marriage market

But a better example of the effect of the authorities' action followed an order published in November 1686 by the Commissioners for the Diocese of London, who were acting whilst the Bishop, Henry Compton was under suspension. The order was against 'the pretended exemptions of the Parishes of Trinity Minories, St James Duke Place and St Botolph Aldgate'. At the end of January 1686/7 these Commissioners published another order forbidding clandestine weddings on pain of suspension. Perhaps it was no coincidence that on 29 January 1686/7 a new register commenced at the Minories and this was marked by a temporary halt in the number of weddings: only twenty-one are recorded there in the next month, about one-third of the expected number. Adam Elliott, Rector of Duke's Place, was suspended from his living for three years from 17 February 1686/7 by the Commissioners for the Diocese of London.[22] But strangely, Elliott's suspension had no additional impact in suppressing the marriage trade at the Minories. In fact from mid-March the volume of marriages returned to its former level and business was particularly brisk during April and May while Elliott remained suspended. However, the suppression of Duke's Place was matched by a resurgence in the number of weddings carried out in other parishes in London and its suburbs and during 1687 the number of marriage licences issued by the Bishop of London's Registry also more than doubled to 351. The pattern of weddings at Cripplegate, for instance, graphically shows how the level of marriages at individual churches was affected by events at the clandestine centres, the number of weddings in 1687 rising sharply *(see Figure 2 above).*

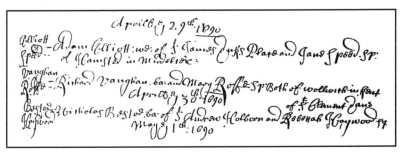

Figure 3: Wedding of Adam Elliott, Rector of St James Duke's Place at Holy Trinity Minories 29 April 1690 (Illustration courtesy of Guildhall Library, Corporation of London, Ms 9244 and GL Ms 9244 thereafter)

But when, after just three months suspension, Elliott was reinstated to his living on appeal on 28 May 1687, the clandestine trade was quickly re-established at Duke's Place and other centres such as St George Southwark. The number of weddings at Duke's Place soon reached and surpassed its former level, whilst marriages at other London churches correspondingly fell back, as did the number of licences issued. In fact the clandestine trade restarted with renewed vigour at the two main centres: at the Minories the peak years were 1691, when 1,000 weddings are recorded, and the following year with 1,060 noted, whilst at Duke's Place the number of weddings rose to 1,803 in 1690.

OTHER CLANDESTINE CENTRES

The Minories and Duke's Place were not the only clandestine centres, but their scale of activities completely dwarfed that at other venues. Nevertheless at many churches and chapels a few hundred weddings were performed annually, compared to a couple of dozen which might otherwise have been expected under regular arrangements.

St Pancras Middlesex became a noted clandestine centre during Randolph Yearwood or Yarwood's incumbency which started in 1655. Yearwood had a series of running battles with his parishioners and vestry over payment to him of rents and tithes, which led him to take proceedings in the Court of the Exchequer for their recovery. His lack of income may have been the initial spur to his entry into the clandestine market and his continuing misfortunes may have made it necessary to continue. It is probable that in 1675 his unpaid legal expenses were the reason for his arrest on three actions for debt and his confinement in the Fleet debtors' prison the following year. Then one of his parishioners William Turbett prosecuted him in the Court of the Dean and Chapter of St Paul's for marrying a couple in October 1674 without banns or licence. The proceedings were prolonged, lasting on and off from 1676 to 1684, including an appeal to the Court of Arches. Yearwood was suspended for three years by the Dean and Chapter and ordered to pay Turbett's costs, which he failed to do, leading to further legal wrangling.

The register for St Pancras contains a detailed note made in 1689 after Yearwood's death by the incoming incumbent Dr John Marshall who recorded that during the time of his predecessor's incumbency there had been

> strange times of liberty. Mr Yearwood was put often under suspension and there were severall persons that attended here purely to marry people, and it was a perfect scramble who should get to perform ye office and ... they would not register them, but to those that desires them they sometimes gave certificates under their hands.[23]

Such was the chaos that after 1669 the registers were only irregularly kept and pages were torn out. Even before this, registration was imperfect as the May 1665 entry for the marriage of 'The ostler and servt maid at ye Kings Head in Smithfields' testifies!

Dr Marshall attempted to make good some of the loss by transcribing details kept by the clerk 'for his own satisfaction' of those weddings at which he was present from about 1683 or 1684 and also those details which

> Mr Yearwood sett down in his pocket book or Almanack, where I am informed he used to put down those Marriages wch. he celebrated, some at his lodgings in London, & some here in Church or Chappell.

Despite Marshall's efforts, records of hundreds or even thousands of ceremonies must have been lost or went unrecorded. Marshall also notes that 'tis to be feared that interest & partiality (in ye Clerk) made him enter some that really were not marryed'.

It is not clear whether subsequent incumbents at St Pancras shared Marshall's strictly correct approach or whether he himself was able to prevent all abuses. In 1691, for instance, the register records a wedding where 'both parties went by wrong names and yt ye man afterwards married another woman' while in 1704 appears 'a marriage surreptitiously solemnized by Mr Dunkin wtt my knowledge or leave'. It is questionable whether in 1700 Congreve was describing a current or past situation when he wrote that there was 'such coupling at Pancras that they stand behind one another as 'twere a country dance'. But there can be less doubt about a newspaper report in 1718 which represented the church as one where couples could marry at cut-price rates without a regular licence; the Vicar was then one Edward de Chair.[24]

St Botolph Aldgate, a neighbour of Holy Trinity Minories and Duke's Place, carried out a clandestine trade which seems to have been considerably better regulated than was St Pancras under Yearwood. However, the activities at this church did not escape the attentions of the Bishop of London, for the register notes on 12 December 1684 that 'Here followeth the marriages by bannes and lycences there being none to be married without', going on to note that the King (Charles II)

> hath conveyed and transferred all power he had of visiting the Minister and church ... to the Lord Bishopp of London and Sr Thomas Exton his Chancellor.

During the following year (1685) there were only 75 weddings at the church compared to an annual average of 175 in the previous five years, with a further fall to 53 marriages in 1687, the year of Adam Elliott's suspension. However by 1691 the marriage trade had been re-established with around 200 weddings per year, and a peak of 285 in 1698. In most years after that there were between 100 and 150 marriages, before the trade started to decline around 1725.

Another nearby clandestine centre was at St Katherinc by the Tower where the number of marriages rose from around 60 a year in the 1630s to 90 annually in the 1660s, an average of 322 per year in the late 1670s and 470 in the 1680s. Under a charter dating from the reign of Henry VI the precincts of the Royal Hospital and collegiate church of St Katherine by the Tower

> were declared exempt, free and quit for all jurisdiction, secular and ecclesiastical, except that of the Lord Chancellor of England.

The chapel was served by three 'brothers' in weekly turns. During the 1680s one of these brothers, Edward Lake DD, was non-resident and in his absence Robert Garrett served two weeks at a time and received the fees due to Lake (Garrett was reduced to serving for one week from April 1685). Unfortunately, Garrett was less than scrupulous about recording the weddings he carried out: throughout 1685 and 1686 there are recurring references to non-registration during Garrett's turn, the following entry being typical:

> Mr Garretts weake begun Sunday ye 30 August [1685] and ends Saterday ye
> 5 September in the weake seven weddings but none registered here.

In 1686 Garrett came into opposition with the newly-appointed Master of the Hospital, Sir James Butler, who suspended him, the register for 14 November 1686 noting his suspension. From the following week, 21 November 1686, the register notes 'ye first week of licences', a separate register recording the issue of allegations by the resident 'brother'. Henceforth, the register seems to record all marriages carried out, although a visitation of 1691/2 suggested there were continuing irregularities and two of the brothers were suspended. The marriage trade only became properly regulated after a visitation by the Lord Chancellor, Lord Somers, to investigate alleged misconduct by the Master; in consequence a range of new procedures was introduced for running the hospital, including the conduct of marriages.[25]

Other churches to the east of London were also popular marriage venues in the 1670s and 1680s, notably St Mary Bromley, St Leonard and nearby St Mary Stratford Bow. At St Dunstan Stepney, a popular venue before the Civil War, the parson had been able to issue marriage licences from at least 1669, and did so in large numbers.

But clandestine and irregular marriages were not only confined to the area on the eastern fringes of the City. The level of marriages at St George Southwark steadily increased throughout the seventeenth century and remained in the range 200-400 weddings annually in the 1660s and 1670s. The most likely explanation is that the parish traded on its nearness to the area known as the 'Rules' of the King's Bench Prison. At nearby St Saviour Southwark the weddings of large numbers of non-resident couples are recorded in the register; two-thirds of those marrying there in 1660, for instance, came from outside the parish.[26]

To the north of the City at Cripplegate, the chapel of the Clothworkers Company, known as Lamb's Chapel, became a popular venue in the early 1700s and evidently dabbled with the clandestine trade: the chapel register reveals that in December 1706

> Revd Mr Charles Badham chosen Reader of Lambs Chapel in place of Mr Wild removed for marrying witht Bans or Licence.

Less than three years later, in June 1709, Badham was himself removed, along with the clerk George Wilson, for committing the same offence.[27]

LEGISLATION IN THE 1690s

There were several attempts to put an end to clandestine weddings in the early 1690s but these failed to make any impact as they lacked the backing of supporting legislation. These attempts also aroused opposition and, for instance, in 1692 the parish vestry at the Minories vigorously pledged to pay their share of any costs to preserve their privileges 'against all opposers whatsoever'. The first serious attempt to regulate marriages came with an Act in 1694 (5 & 6 William and Mary c.21, 1693/4) primarily to raise revenue for the war against France which, amongst other things, introduced a tax of 5s. on every marriage licence or certificate to be issued. In itself this had no noticeable impact but it paved the way for a further Act (6 & 7 William and Mary c.6, 1694) which attempted to raise additional revenue for the war effort by imposing Stamp Duty Tax on a sliding scale for all births, marriages and deaths. The most effective clause was that which enacted

> that noe person shall bee married att any place pretending to be exempt from the visitation of the Bishop of the Diocese without a licence first had and obtained except the banns shall be spoken and certified according to law.

A fine of £100 was levied against 'parsons, curates and vicars' who married couples other than as the Act intended.

This Act, which became effective on 1 May 1695, affected fundamentally the activities at the Minories. From the next day, the Minories marriage register notes that all weddings were either by licence or after banns. Evidently the Bishop of London authorised the rector of the Minories to act as a surrogate able to issue marriage licences and, as Tomlinson notes, 'in this way the incumbent and the parishioners were, in some degree, compensated for the inevitable loss'. From June 1695 copies of allegations taken by the incumbent John King start to appear regularly in the Bishop of London's records. However, in spite of this, the number of weddings at the Minories fell sharply to 477 in 1695.

But as an unintended consequence the Act led to a greater diversity in the London marriage market, as it appeared to allow the interpretation that weddings were perfectly valid so long as they were supported by a properly sanctioned licence, without any recognition of the residential requirement in the canons of 1604. It is noticeable that the earliest registers for two important chapels close to the City – those at Lincoln's Inn and Gray's Inn – start from 1 May 1695 recording weddings by licence, exploiting the apparent legislative loophole. At other churches the implementation of the Act was marked by greater detail appearing in the marriage register. This was the case at St Katherine by the Tower where a new register began on 1 May 1695, noting parishes and occupations of those marrying. Similarly at St George Southwark, already noted as a clandestine centre, the parishes of those marrying were given for the first time; the same is apparent at St Mary Whitechapel, also a popular marriage venue. Two City parishes – St Margaret Lothbury and St Peter le Poer – also started to record parish of origin at this time, whilst St Antholin Budge Row commenced a new register in May 1695. At St Botolph Aldgate, where by now the clandestine trade had apparently resumed, a new register also commenced from 1 May 1695 even though there was space in the existing register.[28] It seems likely that then or shortly afterwards the Aldgate curate, Edward Jones, was empowered to grant licences as records of marriage allegations issued from that church survive in the Bishop of London's series from 8 February 1695/6.

But although that Act had some obvious impact, it did not bring about the intended end of the clandestine trade. To tighten things up, a further Act (7 & 8 William III c.35, 1695) was passed. In its preamble this indicates how the intention of the earlier Act had been evaded

> and made of none effect by several parsons, vicars and curates who to avoid the said penalty of £100 do substitute and employ and knowingly and wittingly suffer and permitt diverse other ministers to marry great numbers of persons in their respective churches and chapels without publication of banns or licences of marriage.

The new Act provided that from 24 June 1696 the £100 penalty applied equally to anyone carrying out such ceremonies, not just the incumbent, whilst those married in this way were themselves liable to a £10 fine.

Just like its predecessor, the effect of the 1696 Act can be noted in parish registers. At Lamb's Chapel, Cripplegate (later St James in the Wall) the register dates from the day following the Act (25 June 1696) whilst that for Aske's Hospital Chapel, Hoxton, dates from the same year. Even the register of the Fleet Prison Chapel (see p. 29 below) notes from 25 June 1696 'Marriages by licence from Docters Comuns'. From 1696 the Westminster

Abbey register started to note the parishes of those marrying, while Sir Christopher Wren's partly-completed St Paul's Cathedral started to take advantage of the marriage trade when services began there in 1697: both these latter two venues became popular marriage choices for the gentry.

The amending legislation introduced in 1696 had the required effect at Duke's Place, which seems to have been one of those centres which had made the previous Act 'of none effect'. It is perhaps significant that from 13 July 1696, just two weeks after the Act took effect, the marriage register starts to note more systematically the origins of those marrying, perhaps to reflect the greater openness under which the parish was forced to act. Marriages there were almost certainly by licence after this, although it seems that Adam Elliott's earlier transgressions were not forgiven: before 1700 it seems probable that couples marrying there had to obtain a licence either from the Bishop's or Archbishop's Registry. Only after Elliott's death in 1700 and the institution of his successor John Grafty, were marriage allegations issued directly from Duke's Place itself.

Further impetus to the need to record relevant details of those marrying came from yet another Act (9 William III c.32) 'for preventing frauds & abuses in the charging, collecting & paying the Duties upon marriages, baptisms, burials, bachelors and Widows' which came into effect on 1 August 1698. For marriages this required recording 'the place of abode of the several husbands upon pain ... of £20' and also 'the respective Degree, condition or Quality according to his majesties duty'.

In effect, the clandestine nature of many marriages had been eliminated and most weddings in these centres from 1695 are probably best described as irregular. But if the authorities thought that these changes meant that the threat of clandestine marriage had been banished they were wrong, for the Fleet, the most notorious of the clandestine centres, was about to come into its own.

FLEET MARRIAGES

The Fleet marriages have been described in detail by Steel and Brown in recent decades and I only propose to sketch in a little of the general background here. Some marriages had been carried out in the prison chapel from the early 1600s but the Fleet was only regarded as a clandestine centre later in the seventeenth century. It claimed to be exempt from the bishop's jurisdiction because the wardenship of the prison was in private hands and only the Crown had the right to visitation. But even if the bishop had no right of access, the opposite was generally true for anyone else, as there was open and unrestricted access to the prison for anyone wishing to visit.

The legislation of the 1690s, which started to curtail the clandestine trade elsewhere, proved to be a stimulus to the Fleet. The legislators were aware of marriages taking place at the Fleet for the Act introduced in 1696 specifically referred to 'diverse ministers in prison for debt & otherwise do marry in the said prisons'.

The prison wardens regarded the prison as a commercial enterprise and openly condoned the expanding marriage trade as they could profit both from a share of the fees and from the business that couples marrying brought to the places of entertainment within the prison confines. One of these places was known as Bartholomew Fair after Bartholomew Bassett, clerk to the prison chaplain. Bassett had the lease of the prison kitchen and eating-house and the nickname was intended to signify a place of ill-repute: the original Bartholomew Fair was held in the market of Smithfields on the Feast of Bartholomew (24 August) renowned as a scene of low entertainments, including exhibitions of monsters. The Fleet chaplain, Robert Elborrow, himself officiated at some clandestine weddings but more usually married by banns or licence. However, it was said in 1705 that he was 'an ancient man' who 'under a colour doth allow his clerk to do what he pleases'.

Other early Fleet parsons were Nehemiah Rogers, active from 1697 and himself a Fleet debt prisoner from 1700/1, who was still able to continue as Rector of Ashingdon, Essex until deprived of his living in 1706, and James Coulton, a Cambridge graduate and naval chaplain who was Rector of Stambridge, Essex until he too was deprived in 1704 by the Bishop of London for performing clandestine marriages 'and other ill practices'. These clergy usually carried out the wedding ceremonies in the prison chapel, paying the chaplain Elborrow or Bassett his clerk a shilling for the courtesy.[29]

As Brown indicates, using the evidence of what maybe the earliest authentic Fleet register, the number of weddings almost doubled during 1695 only to fall back from 25 June 1696 as the Fleet conformed to the new legislative requirements. As mentioned above, from that date, the register notes that marriages were by licence from Doctors' Commons and the individual entries confirm that of the 140 weddings recorded in 1697 some 119 were noted as by licence issued under the Archbishop's authority, only nine were from the Bishop of London and the remainder were after banns.[30]

The number of Fleet marriages continued to fall the next year (1698) but as the likelihood of prosecution faded, the clandestine trade returned. Brown estimates that some 2,250 Fleet weddings were celebrated in 1700, perhaps a third of the London marriage trade, almost equal to the former level at Duke's Place and the Minories.

In spite of the Fleet's claims to exemption, an ecclesiastical visitation was allowed in 1702. This made some attempt to regulate proceedings at the Fleet and one result was that one Thomas Bassett swore not to marry without banns or licence unless recommended by a justice in the case of a 'big belly'. This visitation also referred to the above-mentioned James Coulton as marrying couples 'in and around the Fleet gate and all the Rules over' – the 'Rules' being the area surrounding the prison where many debt prisoners were allowed to live due to overcrowding in the prison itself. By 1710 the marriage trade had already substantially moved from the prison chapel to houses in the Rules. Registers survive for two of these marriage-houses, that for King dating from September 1706 and Henry Tuftin's register commencing in August 1709. In June 1712 legislation (10 Anne c.19) came into effect which speeded up this process of marriage outside the prison, for henceforth prison-keepers were to be fined if they allowed marriages on their premises. A month before the Act took effect John Lilley, turnkey of the prison, had established his chapel at the Bull & Garter adjacent to the prison; Thomas Hodgkins, apparently clerk to the prison chapel, had similarly set up a chapel in Fleet Lane. The development of these outlets was undoubtedly an important boost to the marriage trade: not only was there no longer the stigma of being within the prison walls, but also the marriage-houses were in a prominent position within an area which had better facilities.

Few parsons had sufficient capital to set up their own marriage-houses so they had to depend on marriage-house-keepers to provide the necessary facilities, usually a room set aside specifically for weddings to take place and called a chapel. Some marriage-houses kept a resident parson, particularly in the period before 1730: Joshua Lilley for instance advertised that at the Hand & Pen by Fleet Ditch marriages were performed 'by a Gentleman regularly bred at one of our Universities and lawfully ordained'. By the 1730s the numbers of marriage-houses had increased and the number of clergy reduced. The stronger bargaining position of the clerics meant that they could make better agreements. Some had an agreement which guaranteed business with a particular house but which gave them the right to also marry elsewhere, even in their own house or much further afield. One of the leading parsons Walter Wyatt carried out most of his trade at the houses of Harling and Wheeler in 1737 but in 1745 he was involved mainly at three other houses as well as operating on a freelance basis around the numerous houses and taverns which catered for this blossoming trade. Wyatt's income at this time exceeded £500 per year.

By the 1720s over 4,000 Fleet weddings were taking place annually, while by the 1740s well over half of London marriages, some 6,500 each year, were at the Fleet, with a further thousand weddings conducted at Alexander Keith's Mayfair Chapel.

Alexander Keith had been appointed as chaplain at the Mayfair Chapel, a proprietary chapel in Curzon Street in the parish of St George Hanover Square, sometime before 1728. Keith's continued employment there depended very much on the numbers he could attract by his preaching, for he had no security of tenure and could be dismissed with little or no notice. Although his appointment did not allow him to conduct weddings and any fees properly belonged to the incumbent of St George, nevertheless it seems likely that soon after he took over there he started his matrimonial business. He conducted 442 weddings in 1730 but after two successful years it appears that he was virtually forced out of business by Dr Trebeck, Rector of St George's, whose fees had fallen drastically as a result. After lying low for some years Keith resumed his activities in 1741, marrying 743 couples the next year. Dr Trebeck brought an action against Keith, but even when the latter was sent to the Fleet Prison on a writ of excommunication for his matrimonial offences, trade at the chapel continued unabated, carried out by

Fleet parsons on his behalf, with licences which Keith had signed. In the six years before Hardwicke's Act, his chapel became the major clandestine centre outside the Fleet: over 6,600 weddings were conducted there during this period, over 1,000 in each year on average. On the final day before Hardwicke's Act became law, no less than sixty-one weddings were performed there.[31]

THE FLEET REGISTERS AND NOTEBOOKS

The need for a public record had meant that even the most clandestine of marriages, including those at the Fleet, were properly recorded in registers kept for this purpose, even though some entries were not to be revealed to enquirers. Such registers were even produced as evidence in court cases, which is how two Fleet registers are to be found amongst probate records at the Public Record Office. The Public Record Office is also the storehouse for the most significant source of clandestine marriages, the Fleet registers and notebooks. A widely-read guide to the records there advises would-be searchers that

> the Fleet Registers should be treated with extreme caution as the dates given are unreliable, and names, indeed whole entries may be fictitious'.[32]

It is perhaps understandable that the authors sounded a warning note about entries in the Fleet registers and notebooks. Burn's original work on the registers and subsequent descriptions place considerable emphasis on, and give numerous examples, of the notoriety and abuses characterising Fleet marriages which led to Lord Hardwicke's Act of 1753.

However, generally, the Fleet parsons took pains to make marriage ceremonies seem as legal and solemn as possible in the circumstances. Most parsons usually avoided marrying those, such as minors, whose nuptial activities might later lead to enquiries or legal proceedings. 'Official' marriage certificates were issued, some bearing the royal coat of arms, although these had no legal validity as they were not stamped with the requisite 5s. stamp duty. Lilley, who designated himself 'Clerk of the Fleet', let it be known that his certificates were approved by the Lord Mayor of London, whilst another parson Mottram incorporated the City arms on his certificates, which described the place of marriage as either St Bride Fleet Street, St Martin Ludgate or St Sepulchre according to the location of the marriage-house where the wedding was conducted.

Nevertheless there were numerous and frequent abuses. Many weddings were conducted outside the required hours of eight a.m. to noon; sometimes it is recorded that the parson was called from his bed to marry a couple. Ceremonies were performed as quickly as possible, covering only the bare essentials of the prayer book, and multiple weddings often took place. It was also frequently claimed that certificates were issued even though no ceremony had been performed, whilst 'sham marriages' were practised, such as where a woman in debt married a man to give her financial freedom, as her debts contracted before marriage automatically transferred to her husband. It was claimed 'that there are men provided there who have each of them, within the compass of a year, married several women for this wicked purpose'. The flagrant activities of the 'plyers', whose trade depended on procuring couples to marry at a particular house, also caused public outrage and concern.

On the whole most registers of the marriage-houses and parsons were maintained in better order than many found in the established church at the same period. Most Fleet registers record more detail than is customary in many other London registers of this period, containing the vital details of the origins of bride and groom, more often than not giving the groom's occupation as well. 'Parson' Gaynam claimed, with some justification, that his register was 'as fair a register as any church in England can produce'. However, it was common knowledge that the keeping of many registers was open to abuse. Backdated entries, probably to legitimize a pregnancy or regularize a long-standing common law union, occasionally occurred with entries inserted in gaps or blank pages in the earlier part of registers. More unusually, Beric Lloyd's research has provided definite evidence of forged and backdated registers, showing that parts of RG 7/2 which purport to date from 1675-1679 actually date from 1738-1747. Mark Herber's recent research verifies and extends Lloyd's findings. A wholesale forgery of this kind has little practical use, except in providing a register for which search fees could be later levied.[33]

From an archivist's point of view the registers and notebooks remain unauthenticated and without a clearly documented provenance: Burn outlines how they remained in private hands for nearly seventy years from the demise of the Fleet, passing through a number of owners, until they were purchased from one William Cox by the Government in 1821 for £260 6s. 6d. They were then deposited in the office of the Registrar of the Consistory Court of London, ultimately passing into the Public Record Office's care.

However, these genuine concerns about provenance, and the undoubted abuses, need to be balanced against what is by now clearly overwhelming evidence that the vast majority of entries in the 290 volumes of registers and indexes, and the 540 or so notebooks, represent the weddings of a significant proportion of the population of London, its suburbs and the surrounding counties. Stephen Hale has estimated that the registers probably contain some 400,000 entries, representing 220,000 weddings: many weddings are duplicated in several registers. More recently Mark Herber estimates that the registers and notebooks contain around 350,000 entries.[34]

From details in the registers it is evident that the Fleet catered for a complete cross-section of London people, from the very rich to the very poor. Brown's analysis shows that by far the largest group of grooms were craftsmen of one sort or another with between 33% and 43% in each of the years studied, while up to the 1720s at least, sailors were the second largest group with over a quarter of grooms so-described in 1710 but only 8% (one in twelve) in 1740. Tradesmen and innkeepers and farmers, husbandmen and others in agricultural occupations were the next most common, both groups accounting for around one in ten Fleet customers in any year (*see Figure 4*).

My own notes on Essex marriages show that, for the large numbers travelling to London from the surrounding counties, there was a greater tendency for the better sort – farmers, tradesmen and craftsmen – to marry there. At Holy Trinity Minories between 1698 and 1713, of 112 Essex grooms whose occupations were given in the registers, 51 (45%) were in farming occupations (mostly described as husbandmen), 28 (25%) worked in either clothing or building crafts, 13 were tradesmen of various kinds,

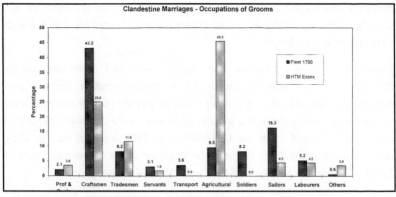

Figure 4: Occupations of grooms at the Fleet (1700) compared to Essex grooms at Holy Trinity Minories (1698-1713)

Figure 5: A Rake's Progress 'Invented Painted and Engrav'd by Wm Hogarth and Publish'd June ye 24 1735'
This depicts the marriage at St Marylebone of the Rake and his old, rich bride. According to J.Ireland (Hogarth Illustrated
– 1791) at that time Marylebone church was then considered as 'at such a distance from London as to become the
usual resort of those who wished to be privately married'
Illustration by courtesy of the Trustees of Sir John Soane's Museum.

with the remaining 20 spread across a range of occupations, rich or poor. Figure 4 compares the occupational profile for such Essex grooms at the Minories to the general profile for Fleet marriages.

Confirmation of the relative importance of the Fleet weddings among the working population of London was recently provided by the work of social historian David Kent. His detailed study of the settlement examinations for St Martin-in-the-Fields reveals that 59% of those seeking a settlement there in 1750/1 had been married at the Fleet.[35]

The evidence increasingly shows that the long-standing and commonly-expressed view about the Fleet marriage registers and notebooks is misleading. With the county indexing initiatives of recent years, and Mark Herber's ambitious indexing project, there is some hope that these 'greatest untapped genealogical sources' may be more accessible in the near future.

MARRIAGE BY LICENCE

It is apparent from the account above that by at least 1700 the three Aldgate churches of Holy Trinity, Duke's Place and St Botolph were each able to issue marriage licences and were now irregular rather than clandestine centres. Partly as a result of them gaining this right, the number of marriage licences issued under the Bishop of London's authority more than trebled from under 200 a year between 1691 and 1695 to well over 600 annually in the next five years. Of these, only around a third each year seem to have been issued from the Registry and the rest by the surrogates at Stepney and the Aldgate churches. The increase in the number of licences from the Bishop's Registry clearly dates from the implementation of the 1695 Act; just 37 licences had been issued from the registry in the six months before 1 May 1695 whereas 42 were granted in May 1695 alone and 168 in the following twelve months.

In addition to the Aldgate churches, within a few years the incumbents of Allhallows London Wall and St Martin-in-the-Fields also gained the right to act as surrogates for the Bishop. At St Dunstan Stepney from 1695 the number of Stepney weddings rose fourfold from under 150 in 1695 to over 600 each year after that – an obvious reflection of the lessened dominance of the Minories and Duke's Place.

From the government's point of view the Acts of 1695 and 1696 had the intended effect of raising the level of marriage by licence and thereby revenue. The French visitor Misson noted in 1697 that it was the desire to avoid the calling of banns that led to a large number of the middling sort of London people marrying by licence as

> very few are willing to have their affairs declar'd to all the world in a publick place, when for a guinea they may do it snug, and without noise ... Thus then, they buy what they call a Licence, and are marry'd in their Closets, in presence of a couple of Friends, that serve for witnesses.[36]

The unintended consequence of the legislation in creating a wider diversity in the London marriage business seems to have been helped by the church authorities' willingness to condone a greater degree of irregular marriage by licence and to ignore the letter of canon law. Misson also observed 'my good Friends the Clergy, who find their accounts in it, are not very zealous to prevent it'. No doubt the church recognised that these marriages generated a considerable amount of licence fees now that the main clandestine threat from the Aldgate centres had been suppressed.

Figure 6 Marriage licence allegations enrolled in the Faculty Office increased significantly after 1695.

As I have already mentioned, from 1695 there was a marked growth in marriages by licence, particularly at churches where the clergyman was able to issue marriage licences on the spot. As the clandestine trade focused on the Fleet in the early 1700s, another fashionable trend developed in parallel among the middle classes: irregular marriage at a London church by licence issued from the Archbishop of Canterbury's offices in Doctors' Commons in Knightrider Street. In theory licences from the Faculty Office were only needed where one of the partners came from the 'Northern Province' and the other from the south, and could be used for marriages throughout the country. Similarly, licences from the Vicar General were really only needed where the bride and groom came from different dioceses within the Province of Canterbury. In both cases the church canons still required the wedding to be held in the parish church or chapel of either bride and groom 'and in no other place'. This was nearly always ignored: both of these issuing offices (and that of the Bishop of London) were prepared to grant licences for marriage to take place anywhere that the parties chose. At the Faculty Office, where the number of licences issued had hovered around the 300 mark during the 1680s (apart from a brief rise during Elliott's suspension in 1687) business more than doubled from 1 May 1695, reaching 617 licences that year, 762 in 1696, and just below 1,000 in each of the next two years. The level then abated slightly in the next few years, falling to 583 in 1702, before the pattern of increase resumed, with the number of licences climbing to 1,074 in 1714 (see Figure 6).[37] This growth seems to have been something of a counterbalance to the Fleet clandestine trade, for marriages by licence from either the Faculty Office or Vicar General's Office became the fashion among the middle classes. In London it became the practice for such marriages to take place in the churches close to Doctors' Commons, the main beneficiaries from this trade being the churches of St Benet Paul's Wharf, St Mary Magdalen Old Fish Street and St Gregory by St Paul.

Marriages at the above churches seem to have captured the imagination from 1705 onwards. At St Benet there were only about 30 weddings a year before 1705 but in the next five years this grew to an annual average of 200 marriages. From 1712 onwards there was a marked and sustained increase with 302 weddings recorded that year, with a further steady growth to a peak of 569 weddings in 1724. Trade remained buoyant until a steady reduction can be detected from the early 1730s, the twenty years preceding Hardwicke's Act when Fleet marriages were at their height. Weddings fell to 310 in 1735, 197 in 1746 with only 124 weddings in 1753, the last full year before Hardwicke's Act came into effect when the church's role as a marriage centre ceased overnight. Only six weddings were celebrated there in the nine months after the Act took effect, with just 12, 17 and 16 unions in each of the next three years (see Figure 7). It is perhaps not realised that the

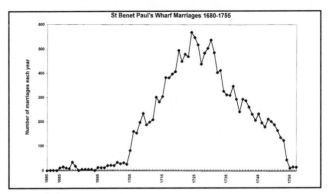

Figure 7 Marriages at Benet Paul's Wharf and other nearby churches were at a peak around 1725-30 but then declined as the Fleet gained supremacy.

1753 Act not only put a stop to clandestine weddings at the Fleet but also had a significant impact on the activities (and income) of certain London churches like St Benet which had enjoyed the benefits of a lucrative trade in irregular marriages by licence.

RURAL IRREGULAR MARRIAGE

It has long been recognised that the abuse of the licence arrangements was not confined to London. It was remarked in a case before the Court of King's Bench in 1794 that

> by the 26th Geo II (Hardwicke's Act of 1753) the evidence of the fact of marriage is more easily obtained than it was before when people wandered up and down the country marrying wherever they pleased.

Some local marriage centres developed in peculiars where the incumbent was able to grant marriage licences. As Cox noted, one such place was the Chapel of Peak Forest, Derbyshire, where in 1728 a 'new register book was purchased and endorsed Foreign Marriages ... These foreign marriages averaged about sixty a year'.[39] Other high incidences of marriages by licence have been noted in towns and cities where marriage licences could be issued. At St Nicholas Rochester, Kent, nearly three-quarters of the weddings between 1727 and 1754 (554 of the 751) were by licence: Rochester was the seat of a bishop. At Holy Trinity Stratford-upon-Avon, Warwickshire, around 40% of marriages in the half-century before Hardwicke's Act were by licence: here the vicar was a surrogate of the Bishop of Worcester.

There is some evidence that clandestine weddings in the provinces could be as shady as those at the Fleet – Jean Cole's study of Wiltshire settlement examinations has uncovered examples. For instance, the examination of John Cripps, labourer of Bradford-on-Avon in 1758, revealed that twenty-eight years previously he had been married to Alice Hubert of Bradford at the sign of the Raven in Bath by a person unknown who read over the ceremony of the Church of England and performed that of the ring.[40]

Perhaps the most extensive analysis by a family historian on rural marriage practice was Colin Harris's study of weddings in Oxford before 1754 arising from the Oxfordshire FHS marriage index project.[41] Harris estimated that in the period from 1660 to 1754 almost three-quarters of the 10,000 weddings in Oxford were by licence. Harris indicated that the

> Oxford City parish registers are full of irregular marriages of couples who came not only from villages throughout Oxfordshire, but also from north Berkshire and west Buckinghamshire.

The reason was that Oxford was the base for church officials granting licences on behalf of the Bishop of Oxford, the Archdeacon of Oxford, the Archdeacon of Berkshire, as well as many of the Berkshire, Buckinghamshire and Oxfordshire peculiar courts. The Bishop of Oxford's Registry was at the back of the church of St Mary Magdalen which itself celebrated 2,655 weddings between 1692 and 1754, nearly all of them for couples from outside the parish; such couples were usually married on the same day that the licence was issued. Even though neither the Archdeacon of Berkshire nor the officials of these peculiar courts had any jurisdiction within the city, this was conveniently ignored: for instance the registers of parishes near the Archdeacon of Berkshire's Registry have many entries for Berkshire people. Harris's research also indicated a further abuse: even where a marriage bond indicated an intended marriage venue outside Oxford, usually the parish of one of the parties, the wedding was still performed in the city. Another practice noted from the end of the seventeenth century was for fellows of Oxford colleges, who also held nearby country livings, to perform weddings for their parishioners in the college chapel. However, it seems that either some of these weddings were never recorded or the registers have not survived.

A similar picture emerges from Stephen Taylor's research for his Ph.D. thesis based on seven rural parishes to the south and west of Reading in the neighbouring county of Berkshire. In addition to the various abuses already noted in Harris's study of Oxford marriages, Taylor's research revealed that marriage by licence was so popular that in some parishes marriage by banns was almost non-existent: somewhere between 73% and 98% of marriages studied were by licence. Taylor used his findings to suggest that aggregative analysis used in family reconstitution studies by historical demographers, which look at marriage-baptism ratios, have been severely distorted by jumbled data arising from the complete freedom that couples had in choosing their marriage venue before Hardwicke's Act. His research also called into question the conclusions of Wrigley's oft-quoted study which drew attention to clandestine weddings 'performed without benefit of church ceremony' in Tetbury, Gloucestershire, which can now be seen to arise from out-of-parish weddings due to an abuse of the licensing system.[42]

DISCUSSION AND CONCLUSIONS

In the introduction I mentioned Don Steel's comments on the great value that the records of clandestine marriages offer for genealogists and family historians. Although some progress has been made in indexing these sources in the three decades since he wrote his comments are as true today as they were then.[43]

The facts speak for themselves. During the 1680s the Minories and Duke's Place accounted for nearly half of all London weddings; hundreds, if not thousands, more took place at other smaller clandestine centres. Throughout the early 1700s the Fleet increased its share and by the 1740s over half of London marriages were at the Fleet or Keith's Mayfair Chapel; in the early 1750s those locations claimed an even larger share. The disrepute which surrounds the Fleet marriages has until recently clouded many scholars' and archivists' vision about this major source. Stone's recent book also falls into the trap of looking only at the unusual cases which ended up before the church courts whilst ignoring the fact that Fleet weddings were virtually the norm for the citizens of London, for people from the London suburbs and from many miles around.[44]

Clandestine or irregular weddings were supposedly secret or hidden but when half the population were indulging in this practice, how could this be so? Towards the end of the seventeenth century it can have been little secret that nearly all the leading families in the parish of South Ockendon, Essex, a rural parish about twenty miles to the east of London, had at least one member married in London. Between 1682 and 1704 there were fourteen weddings at the Minories involving one or other partner from South Ockendon whilst the parish register itself records just thirty-two marriages during the same period. Even two generations later the parish parson was certainly in on the secret when between 1741 and 1754 he recorded in his register that he had received fees for eleven marriages out of parish (of thirty-one weddings listed), some specifically referred to as in London and one has already been traced to the Fleet.

Saving money can hardly have been a factor, not only with the cost of journeying to the City and back, and probably lodging there, but also with the need to pay fees for the ceremony itself and to the local clergyman.[45]

This confirms Boulton's view that 'there is little convincing evidence that ... couples married secretly to save a little money, from religious convictions, to avoid opposition from parents or neighbours or to conceal embarrassing pregnancies'. He goes on to speculate that clandestine marriages may have been 'merely one more "consumption good" devoured by the population after the Restoration' and questions whether they should 'take their place among the latest fashions and consumer durables like pots and china'.[46]

That the clergy were in on the act is also confirmed by a series of weddings of parishioners of West Ham which took place by licence at St Alphage London Wall in the 1730s: both parishes were in the care of the same clergyman, Hugh Wyat. Doubtless other similar instances occurred with clergymen holding more than one cure, marrying their parishioners out of their home parish. Whatever the reason for individual weddings, there is little doubt how widespread clandestine and irregular weddings were in parishes further afield than what is even today outside Greater London.

In addition it is now evident that next to clandestine marriages, the next largest group in London were those by licence, with St Benet Paul's Wharf and other nearby churches flourishing openly for decades as irregular marriage centres. In consequence, between 1695 and 1754 a large proportion of London church marriages should therefore have a corresponding marriage allegation and/or bond in the records at Lambeth Palace or Guildhall Library. Outside London licence marriages were sometimes even more common, as Harris and Taylor have shown.

Not only did Hardwicke's Act put a stop to clandestine weddings at the Fleet and elsewhere, it also ended the common trade in irregular marriages by licence.

This booklet has indicated how sensitive the London and rural marriage trade was to the effects of legislation and probably even to a popular wish to be married in a certain way at a certain place. Family historians researching ancestors in and around London should not be surprised to find a likely marriage at Duke's Place or the Minories in the 1680s, another at St Benet Paul's Wharf a generation later, and an untraced marriage in the 1740s or 1750s which may well turn up after diligent searching in the Fleet registers or notebooks.

The fact that so many of our ancestors' marriages can now be seen as part of a wider, nationwide pattern adds a new dimension to the way that we view what may have been mere names on our family trees.

NOTES

1. Kirk, R, London in 1689/90, Part III, *London and Middlesex Archaeological Society,* NS 6 (1929-33), p.657.

2. Misson, M, *Memoirs and observations in his travels over England* (1719), translated by J.Ozell, pp.183-84.

3. Burn, J S, *History of the Fleet Marriages* (1833); J Ashton, *The Fleet, its River, Prison & Marriages* (1889); D.J.Steel, *National Index of Parish Registers* vol.1: General sources for births, marriages and deaths before 1837 (1968), pp.292-321; R L Brown, 'The rise and fall of the Fleet marriages', in R B Outhwaite, *Marriage and society* (1981), pp.117-36 [this is a distillation of Brown's unpublished MA thesis 'Clandestine marriages in London' (1973). I am grateful to Revd Brown for permission to draw on his works and for his helpful comments on the draft text of this booklet]. A more recent publication is R B Outhwaite, *Clandestine marriage in England 1500-1850* (1995).

4. Steel (1968), op. cit. p.318.

5. Chapman, C R, *Ecclesiastical courts, their officials and their records* (1992) p.6.

6. Outhwaite, R B, *Clandestine Marriage in England 1500-1850* (1995). See also Brown (1981), p.118.

7. Gillis, J R, *For better or worse: British marriages 1600 to the present* (1985) p.17.

8. Laslett, P, *The world we have lost* (2nd edition 1971), pp.149-58.

9. Raine, J, (ed.), Depositions and other ecclesiastical proceedings from the Courts of Durham extending from 1311 to the reign of Elizabeth, *Surtees Society,* vol. 21 (1845). I would like to thank Mr E.Cawte for this reference.

10. Emmison, F G, *Elizabethan life: morals and the church courts* (1974), pp.144-54.

11. Stone, L, *Uncertain unions: marriage in England 1660-1753* (1992).

12. Most recently, Stone (1992), pp.22-23 defines clandestine marriages this way. See also Outhwaite (1995) p.20

13. Kelvin, P, 'The elusive marriage', in *North West Kent Family History Society Journal,* vol.3 no.8, Dec. 1984, pp.259-64. I am grateful to Dr Kelvin for allowing me to adapt the table in her article.

14. Tomlinson, E M, *A history of the Minories* (1907), pp.226-40.

15. Emmison (1974). The 'closed' seasons were from Advent to the Octave of Epiphany, from Septuagesima to the Octave of Easter, and from Rogation Sunday (the 5th Sunday after Easter) to Trinity Sunday.

16. Boulton, J, 'Itching after private marryings? Marriage customs in seventeenth century London', *The London Journal,* vol.16 no.1 (1991), pp.15-29. I would like to thank Dr Jeremy Boulton for permission to draw on his research both in my article 'Marry'd in their closets: clandestine and irregular marriage in London before 1754', *Genealogists' Magazine,* vol.23 no.9, March 1991, and in this booklet.

17. Boulton, J, 'Clandestine marriages in London: an examination of a neglected urban variable', *Urban History,* vol.20 part 2 (October 1993), pp.191-210.

18. Stone (1992) p.20; Gillis (1985) p.89; C Durston, *The family and the English Revolution* (1989), pp.57-86.

19. Tomlinson, op. cit.

20. Phillimore, W P W, and G A Cokayne, *Marriages at St James, Duke's Place, London* (1900-2), 4 volumes; Original registers at Guildhall Library Ms 7894/1-3. Date of register normally given as 1664; the register starts on 24 June 1665 but between entries for 31 December 1665 and 1 January 1665/6 are also recorded three marriages which took place in 1664.

21. Boulton (1993), p.197.

22. The Duke's Place register records that 'there were no marriages from the tenth of March till ye 29th day of May'.

23. Lee, C E, *St Pancras, church and parish* (1955), p.26; G.Tindall, *The Fields Beneath* (1977).

24. W.Congreve, *The way of the world* (1700), Act One. I would like to thank Jean Haynes for drawing attention to this reference which

describes how the couple decided not to delay any longer at Pancras because of the numbers waiting to be married, going instead to Duke's Place where 'they were riveted in a trice'. The 1718 report was in *The Freethinker* and is referred to in Tindall, p.79.

25. Lea, F S, *The Royal Hospital and collegiate church of St Katherine by the Tower* (1878); C Jamison, *The history of the Royal Hospital of St Katherine by the Tower* (1952); *Registers of St Katherine by the Tower,* Harleian Society, vols.75-80. There is considerable overlap in the registers (Guildhall Library Mss 9661-9664); the annotations about Garrett are in Ms 9662.

26. Boulton, J, *Neighbourhood and society: a London suburb in the seventeenth century* (1987), pp.234-35. This is a study of St Saviour Southwark.

27. Noted in registers of Lamb's Chapel, Guildhall Library Ms 1159/1 and 2.

28. The remaining space in this register (Ms 9232/1) was in fact re-used in 1711 when the new register was full.

29. Based on Brown (1973) and (1981).

30. This register RG 7/833 is almost certainly the original register for the Fleet Chapel from 1692 onwards. However, probably because of its small size, it has been classified as one of the Fleet notebooks. It has been transcribed and indexed by S.W.Prentis (1962). The first ten names (from John Alchorne to Thomas Baker) stated to have married by Archbishop's licence have been checked against the relevant British Record Society volumes and all ten such marriages were found to have been issued by the Faculty Office. Of the twenty-three weddings in the register stated to be by bishop's licence, just five appear in the Bishop of London's records. Of these five, three were granted specifically for weddings in the Fleet Chapel, whilst the other two were issued for use at St James Clerkenwell and St Mary Magdalen Old Fish Street respectively.

31. Brown (1973).

32. Bevan, A, *Tracing your ancestors in the Public Record Office* (5th edition 1999), p.7 (the comments quoted originated in the first edition of this book by J Cox and T Padfield, 1981). The PRO Introduction to the RG 7 Class list now gives appropriate recognition to the registers' value.

33. Lloyd, B, *The Fleet forgeries* (typescript, 1987), which shows that parts of RG 7/2 which purport to date from 1675-79 actually date from 1738-47. Lloyd concludes that the earliest Fleet register dates from no earlier than 1691 (see note 30 above). This is explored further and verified in M.Herber *Clandestine Marriages in the Chapel and Rules of the Fleet Prison 1680-1754* (Volume 1 - 1998 and Volume 2 - 1999)

34. I would like to thank Stephen Hale for his agreement to my using his calculations of the volume of Fleet weddings. Hale's index to Fleet marriages for those couples from Kent, Surrey and Sussex border parishes numerous examples of duplicate entries with spelling variations. For instance, the wedding of Richard Bearkin, yeoman of 'Falmborough' Kent and Anne Bearto(n)(p)(s) on 14 December 1717 is recorded in registers RG 7/10, 37, 45, 46 and 47. See also Herber (1998) p.20.

35. D.A.Kent, 'Gone for a soldier: family breakdown and the demography of desertion in a London parish 1750-1791', *Local Population Studies* (Autumn 1990), pp.27-42.

36. Misson (1719).

37. *British Record Society,* vol. 33, Faculty Office Marriage Licences 1632-1714 (1905).

38. M Barber, 'Records of marriage and divorce in Lambeth Palace Library', *Genealogists' Magazine,* vol. 20 no.4 (December 1980), pp.108-17.

39. Cox, J C, *The parish registers of England* (1910), pp.94-95.

40. Jean Cole in correspondence with the author.

41. Harris, C G, 'Marriages in Oxford before 1754', *Oxfordshire Family Historian,* vol.2 no.9 (Autumn 1982), pp.278-85.

42. Taylor, S W, 'Clandestine marriage and clerical practice c.1700-1754, with particular reference to Berkshire' (Unpublished). I would like to thank Dr R M Smith, All Souls College Oxford for providing a copy of this paper.

43. An exception are the indexes to the Holy Trinity Minories marriage registers 1676 to 1754 which have been produced on microfiche by the East of London Family History Society.

[44.] Stone (1992), op. cit.

[45.] Benton, A, 'A perfect scramble – Thurrock marriages in London before 1754', *Panorama* (Journal of the Thurrock Local History Society), 30 (1989).

[46.] Boulton (1993) p.209.

NOTES ON CLANDESTINE AND IRREGULAR MARRIAGE CENTRES

NB. Information regarding churches in the City of London has been extracted from City of London Parish Registers, Guildhall Library Research Guide 4 *(6th edition 1990) with thanks to the Guildhall Library, City of London.*

Fleet registers and notebooks

Originals: Public Record Office, Ruskin Avenue, Kew, Richmond, Surrey TW9 4DU

Registers   1667-1754   RG 7/1-273

(The PRO is reluctant to allow access to the original registers, which must usually be viewed on microfilm at Kew or at the Family Records Centre. This is unfortunate, as the standard of microfilming leaves something to be desired, particularly verso sides and the cutting off of tops of some pages, which renders some page numbers illegible.)

Two registers produced in a probate case are found in PROB 18/50 and mainly cover the period November 1732 to October 1736. Another register, which covers the period March 1725 to January 1731, is in the Bodleian Library Oxford (Rawlinson Ms. 360).

Indexes   RG 7/274-290 (some registers also contain indexes)

Although described as 'indexes' these are, for the most part, 'alphabets' comprising all surnames of grooms only beginning with 'A', but not sorted further, then 'B' etc. throughout the alphabet.

Original notebooks   1692-1754   RG 7/291-835
The main notebook series cover the most prolific parsons and wedding-houses as follows:

Edward Ashwell	October 1733 - July 1740	RG 7/292-386
Burnford	November 1727 - January 1749	RG 7/403-476
William Dare	February 1738 - November 1747	RG 7/479-548
John Gaynam	July 1726 - June 1735	RG 7/589-655
William Wyatt	May 1736 - February 1750	RG 7/679-801

Transcripts and indexes

a) See note 30 above regarding original Fleet Chapel register RG 7/833 from 1691/2-1702, transcribed in S W Prentis, 'Fleet marriages 1691/2-1702' (typescript 1962), copies at PRO Kew, SoG and Guildhall Library.

b) About 2,000 Fleet marriages 1709-1754, extracted from various registers, are in J S Burn, *The Fleet Registers* (1833), pp.94-126; these are indexed in Boyd.

c) B Lloyd, *The Fleet Forgeries* (1987) includes transcripts of parts of RG 7/2 (1675-79) and RG 7/118 (1737/8-1747).

d) M Herber, *Clandestine Marriages in the Chapel and Rules of the Fleet Prison, 1680-1754* contains 1329 entries (Volume 1 – 1998) and 1050 entries (Volume 2 – 1999) respectively, being transcripts or abstracts of the Fleet registers and notebooks in RG 7/3, 118, 162, 163 and 563.

e) S G Hale's unpublished index to Fleet marriages from Kent, Surrey and Sussex, arranged alphabetically and by parish, is available on open shelves at PRO Kew and at the Society of Genealogists.

f) J Parker, Fleet Marriages of Hertfordshire People to 1754: an alphabetical index to grooms and brides *(Hertfordshire Family and Population History Society Special Publication No.2, 1999)* contains an alphabetical index to some 6,500 entries for all traceable Hertfordshire people extracted from all original Fleet registers (but not the notebooks).

Holy Trinity Minories

Original marriage registers: Guildhall Library

1579/80-1644	Ms 9238	Indexed in Boyd's marriage index
1644-48/9	Ms 9241/1	" " " " " " "
1657/8-59	Ms 9242A	" " " " " " "
1660-63	Ms 9241/2	" " " " " " "
1676-83	Ms 9242B	Transcript & index: East of London FHS, vol.1
1683-86	Ms 9243	Index East of London FHS vol.2
1686-92/3	Ms 9244	" " " " " " " " vol.3
1692/3-1754	Ms 9243	" " " " " " " " vols.4 & 5.
1693/4-1713	Ms 9245	Duplicates Ms 9243 (some abbreviation)

Keith's Mayfair Chapel

(also known as St George's Chapel, Mayfair or Hyde Park Corner)

Original Registers (1729-31 and 1735-54): Split between
City of Westminster Archives Centre, 10 St Ann's Street, London SW1P 2XR

1735-44	Volume 1
1744-49	Volume 2
1749-54	Volume 3

Public Record Office, Kew (with Fleet registers and also on microfilm at FRC)

1729-31	RG 7/ 99
1748	RG7/ 178
1747-49 & 1752	RG7/ 221
1748	RG7/ 239
1749-53	RG7/ 248
1753-54	RG7/ 272 & 273.

Printed transcript: Harleian Society, vol.15. Indexed in Boyd's marriage index.

St Benet Paul's Wharf

Original Registers: Guildhall Library

1619-1715	Ms 5716
1715-28	Ms 5718/1
1728-42	Ms 5718/2
1742/3-54	Ms 5718/3

Printed transcripts and indexes:
1618-1730/1   Harleian Society, vol.39 Indexed in Boyd's marriage index
1731-1837   " " " " " ,   vol.40 Indexed (to 1754) in Boyd's
marriage index

St Botolph Aldgate

Original Registers: Guildhall Library
1558-1625	Ms 9220	(for details of duplicate and related records see Guildhall Library Research Guide 4)
1625-56	Ms 9224	Indexed 1593-1640 in Ms 9233
1658-75	Ms 9229	Includes banns 1653-58
1675-95	Ms 9230/1	
1695-1711	Ms 9226	
1711-22	Ms 9230/1	
1722-54	Ms 9230/2	

Transcripts None.   Index 1593-1640 (see above); not
in Boyd

St Dunstan Stepney

Original registers: London Metropolitan Archives, 40 Northampton Road, London EC1R 0HB
1568-1653   Microfilm X24/68
1653-59   Microfilm X24/69
1657-86   Microfilm X24/68
1686-1719   Microfilm X24/68
1719-54   Microfilm X24/23
[Original registers P93/DUN 264-266, 269 and 273 are unfit for production]

Printed transcripts and indexes
                    vol.1 1568-1640   Sir Thomas Colyer-Ferguson
                    vol.2 1640-97   " " " " " " " "
                    vol.3 1697-1719   " " " " " " " "
The above transcripts are indexed in Boyd's marriage index
Transcript and index   1719-54
Typescript by Sir Thomas Colyer-Ferguson (published on microfiche by Kent

FHS, 1985) Photocopy at GLRO: R1102. Indexed in Boyd's marriage index.

St Gregory by St Paul

Original registers: Guildhall Library

1559-1626/7	Ms 10,231
1627-35/6	Ms 10,232
1636-40	Ms 10,233
1641-50	No marriages during church rebuilding
1650/1-87	Ms 10,233
1687-1724	Ms 18,932
1707-9	Ms 18,933 Rough register, some variants to Ms 18,932
1724-49	Ms 18,934
1749-54	Ms 18,935

Transcripts and indexes 1559-1754 Typescript W H Challen vol.11. Indexed in Boyd's marriage index.

Marriage licences 1687-1837 (with St Mary Magdalen Old Fish Street), The Archivist, College of Arms, Queen Victoria St, London EC4V 4BT (by appointment)

St James Duke's Place

Original marriage registers: Guildhall Library
1665-68 (includes 3 marriages from 1664)
and 1678/9-91/2 Ms 7894/1

1692-1700	Ms 7894/2
1700-54	Ms 7894/3

Printed transcripts W P W Phillimore and G A Cokayne, *Marriages at St James Duke's Place, London* (1900-02)

vol. I	1665-31 December 1683	Indexed in Boyd's marriage index
vol. II	1684-31 December 1690	" " " " " " "
vol. III	1691-1700	" " " " " " "
vol. IV	1700-1837	" " " " " " " (up to 1754)

St Katharine by the Tower

Original registers: Guildhall Library
1584-1618	Ms 9,659/1
1618-53	Ms 9,659/2
1653-80	Ms 9,659/3
1680-1735	Mss 9,660-9,666

There is considerable overlap between these latter series of registers – see *Greater London Parish Registers, Guildhall Library Research Guide 5*

Printed transcripts and indexes 1584-1726 Harleian Society, vols. 75-80 Indexed in Boyd's marriage index (to 1625 only).

Typescript 1704-13 W H Challen vol.51.

Marriage allegations 21 November 1686 - 7 April 1689 are in Ms 9664

St Mary Magdalen Old Fish Street

Original registers: Guildhall Library
1539-1638/9	Ms 11,529 Index and transcript: C R Webb vol.40
1639-64	No register survives
1664/5-1712	Ms 10,221
1712-18	Ms 10,222
1718-32	Ms 10,223
1732-54	Ms 10,224

Transcripts 1664/5-1754 W H Challen vol.10. Indexed in Boyd's marriage index

Marriage licences 1687-1837 (with St Gregory by St Paul)
The Archivist, College of Arms, Queen Victoria Street, London EC4V 4BT (by appointment)

St Pancras

Original registers: Greater London Record Office (P90/PAN1)
1660-69	Microfilm X30/1
1672-1754	Microfilm X30/1

(Original registers P90/PAN 1/1-5 are unfit for production)
Transcripts and index: 1660-1754 Typescript W H Challen vol.22. Indexed in Boyd's marriage index.